OUR MISSION CALLING DEMANDS GOING 12,000 MILES
BUT ALSO DEMANDS ENCOUNTERING DIASPORA
PEOPLE GROUPS 12 FEET AWAY. WE SHOULD BE ON
MISSION WITH GOD NO MATTER WHERE WE ARE ...
WHETHER THAT BE WITH PEOPLE IN ANOTHER
COUNTRY OR OUR NEIGHBORS, DIASPORA PEOPLES,
NEXT DOOR.

Also by Bryan K. Galloway

Traveling Down Their Road: A Workbook for Discovering
and Understanding a People's Worldview

The World as They See

Making Meaning: Contextualization in Practice

TESTIMONIALS

"Bryan Galloway is deeply practical, and wonderfully brilliant. He understands the basics of cultural interaction like few do. At the same time, he cares deeply for the least reached peoples of the world, and carries that compassion to the significant diaspora population of North America who need to experience God's love."
—— Linda Bergquist, Church Planting Catalyst, North American Mission Board

"Here is an excellent, yet brief, book to assist in reaching the peoples among us. Galloway has done a wonderful job helping us understand the movement of the nations from God's perspective and our necessary response. This highly practical guide sets forth disciplines that are easily applied in our contexts."
—— JD Payne, pastor, missiologist, author Strangers Next Door: Immigration, Migration, and Mission

"Bryan and I have rubbed shoulders numerous times over the last several years. I can attest from personal observation: he practices in everyday life what he teaches in this helpful book! You have to admire the simplicity and usefulness of the 5-W's and 5-F's. While helpful for the solo reader, this book would be even more valuable for small groups to study, ponder, and put into practice."
—— Larry Stuckey, Coordinator of Diaspora Initiatives, WorldVenture

"Talking about reaching the nations that have scattered throughout the world is relatively easy. Doing something about it is difficult. Two of the greatest difficulties are knowing where to start and what to do. Beginning with the biblical basis of diaspora missions, Bryan Galloway provides a practical tool designed to move Christians from talk to action. His simple strategies and keen insights help believers understand culture and overcome the difficulties involved in diaspora missions. Reaching the Nations should be read and applied by every pastor, missionary, and church member that has a heart for diaspora missions."

—— Trent DeLoach, Lead Pastor, Clarkston International Bible Church and Director, North American Mission Board Send Relief Clarkston Hub

"Bryan Galloway has been helping missionaries around the world connect with diverse peoples for decades. Now Bryan turns his attention to diaspora ministry. Reaching the Nations combines insights from anthropology and sociology with thirty-two years of fieldwork into a missions guidebook that leads the church to connect with immigrants. Thank you, Bryan, for this 21st Century answer to the ancient question, "Who is My Neighbor?""

—— Brent Waldrep, Research Associate for the American Peoples, International Mission Board (IMB)

"Reaching The Nations is a Biblically-based missional handbook that begins with the heart of Jesus as recorded in Scripture and results in concrete steps for reaching the diaspora living among us. The reader will find this book inspiring, challenging, practical and timely. Bryan Galloway brings together the disciplines of missiology and cultural anthropology along with decades of personal experience. Bryan has lived the lifestyle that he advocates in his book. Get ready to embark on a journey to change the world from

your own neighborhood while answering life's greatest calling – to make disciples of all peoples!"
—— Mark Weible, Director of Church Planting, Greater Orlando Baptist Association

"Wow! This book is so practical. Bryan Galloway's expertise, experience and heart for introducing Jesus to all resident people groups in North America is evident throughout the presentation. It is worthy of a second read in order to select suggestions relative to the reader's sphere of influence. The material is biblically based and highly motivational. Bryan was truly led by the Holy Spirit in developing this tool for advancing the Kingdom among the unreached."
—— Jerry Falley, New American Research Specialist, www.yourneighbor.us

"It's hard to imagine someone more qualified than Bryan Galloway to create a practical guide for reaching the nations. He has distilled more than three decades of experience as a missionary, researcher and global strategist into this concise and powerfully insightful handbook. The timeless principles Bryan presents in his Five Disciplines make Reaching the Nations a "go-to" resource for strategy building and missions education."
—— Robert DeVargas, Founder and CEO, Eternal Interactive

"Bryan Galloway is one of the leading experts in mapping and engaging people groups in the mission world. I have worked with him in the overseas setting and now in the USA. This book gives a biblical foundation as to why we must reach the Unreached Peoples in the USA and around the world. Bryan gives the church very practical information

and steps to strategically engage the unreached in our communities, cities and the world. Reaching the Nations is a practical and essential resource for every believer who desires to reach the nations living among them."
—— Bonita K. Wilson, Nations & Neighbors Catalyst,
Knox County Association of Baptists

"Traditionally most American evangelicals have viewed Jesus' command to make disciples of all nations as a command to send out missionaries to the nations. But what happens when God, in His sovereignty, brings the nations to America? Are evangelicals here willing and ready to "do the Great Commission" among their new neighbors who hail from the ends of the earth? In this book Bryan Galloway gives a Biblical perspective on this paradigm shift as well as provides both churches and individuals with a practical, step by step, approach for reaching the nations that God is bringing to America."
—— VW, IMB Affinity Researcher for Southeast Asia

Reaching the Nations

People that Change the World

BRYAN K. GALLOWAY

FIRST EDITION: DECEMBER 2017

Printed in the United States of America.
CreateSpace, Charleston SC
Available from Amazon.com and other online stores. Available on Kindle and other devices

Biblical quotations are from the English Standard Version (ESV). Copyright 2007, 2011, 2016 by Good News Publishers.

ISBN-13: 978-1979938785
ISBN-10: 1979938784

DEDICATION

TO MY FATHER, ZELIOUS GALLOWAY (1929-2017), WHO WAS DEPENDABLE, TAUGHT BY EXAMPLE, ALWAYS GIVING, AND A PRAYING MAN.

CONTENTS

ACKNOWLEDGMENTS

The insights that I have gained over the course of thirty-two years of missionary life are due less to my own merit than to how God has brought many people into my life.

It is not possible to enumerate all of the people I owe a debt of gratitude. With so many people providing advice and mentoring over many years, I often feel as though I am merely sharing their stories, their ideas, and their insight.

INTRODUCTION
WHO IS MY NEIGHBOR?

Just like the "expert in the law" (Luke 10:29) asked Jesus the question, "Who is my neighbor?", more than likely, we too ask the same question.

The advancement of telecommunications, ease of travel in the world, and pluralism are all changing the world at a quickening pace. Cultures are constantly changing with people continually migrating from place to place ever dispersing where they make a living and rest their head. It is estimated that diaspora peoples[1] throughout the world is at an all-time high. The sheer magnitude of the movement[2] of people in the world today and the years to come makes dispersed people a topic of long-term interest, especially for Christians and the Church.

The diaspora are the dispersion of any people from their original homeland. They are often found first-hand in many urban areas throughout the world as cities become more diverse ... socially, ethnically, and linguistically. More specifically, they come as immigrants, refugees, or international students. Diaspora people do life in two places: the country that they presently reside and their homeland. Their ties with their homeland are through a variety of means

---

[1] Throughout this book, the term "diaspora peoples" or "diaspora people" refers to specific people groups who are dispersed from their original homeland. A people group is the largest group through which the gospel can flow without encountering significant barriers of understanding and acceptance.

[2] See Appendix (pages 87-90) for statistics of diaspora peoples.

not necessarily in combination (e.g. political, social, economic, emotional, etc.).

John Lie clearly summarizes how diaspora have their feet in two places at the same time.

> It is no longer assumed that immigrants make a sharp break from their homelands. Rather, premigration networks, cultures, and capital remain. The sojourn itself is unidirectional nor final (Lie 1995, 304).

Diaspora peoples come from all walks of life. They come from other nations than our own. They come as refugees, international students, and immigrants. They work among us as doctors, nurses, engineers, IT related workers, and a plethora of other professions. They are seen playing cricket in parks, found in shopping centers, supermarkets and often worship in their own temples and mosques.

They often cross our paths and we can easily fail to notice the differences that exist between these peoples. We can fail to realize that many speak primary languages at home other than our own mother tongue. Moreover, we can fail to recognize that they are adhering to and practicing uniquely different socio-cultural-religious values.

As a result, we are faced with the same question that the expert in the law asked, "Who is my neighbor?" That question prompts us to ask several other questions.

Who are the people around us that dress different and speak a different language? How did they get here? Where are they from? What religion do they profess? Last, but not least, have they heard a clear and contextualized [3] presentation of the gospel?

We might be hesitant to encounter these neighbors who are different than ourselves.

JESUS NEVER INTENDED US TO LIVE IN A VACUUM SECLUDED AND ISOLATED FROM PEOPLE DIFFERENT FROM OURSELVES.

Instead, he desires us, just like he did (John 1:14, Phil. 2:5-8), to live among the diverse masses and incarnate the gospel both in word and deed.

God has brought the mission field to our doorstep, making missions both there and here. Reaching diaspora peoples "over here" is a way to reach them "over there." As people move, social networks (i.e., the bridges of God) remain. Travel and technological communication easily allow people to remain in touch with their family, friends and their specific people group networks no matter where they may reside.

The practical aspects of what will happen among diaspora come from how willing we are to do a dramatic gospel and culture inventory. Engaging diaspora peoples is not about giving advice or debating on who needs what or how to do

---

[3] A "contextualized gospel message" impacts a people groups worldview valves and assumptions in life by using the people's language and other cultural forms to make sense and meaning of the gospel.

it. Instead, it is about getting one's "hands dirty", doing it, and sharing the good news in all settings – no matter how difficult or uncomfortable we are in that setting.

It is contradictory when the church embodies missions in another country yet neglects to pay attention or even share a message of hope with diaspora peoples next door who are different from their own congregation. Our mission calling demands going 12,000 miles but also demands encountering diaspora peoples 12 feet away. We should be on mission with God no matter where we are ... whether that be with people in another country or our neighbors, diaspora peoples, next door.

THE PRACTICAL ASPECTS OF WHAT HAPPENS AMONG DIASPORA COME FROM HOW WILLING WE ARE TO DO A DRAMATIC GOSPEL AND CULTURE INVENTORY.

Sometimes our greatest challenges [4] are not seeing the opportunities God lays before us. In God's providence, people groups who once were not accessible are now right outside our front door. We have an opportunity to do missions among unreached and the least reached peoples in the world near our own home, being Christ's ambassador as though He is making his appeal through us (2 Corinthians 5:20).

To start, we need more prayer for diaspora peoples. Christians and the church need intentional, organized and

---

[4] For a discussion of challenges, see Appendix on pages 81-88.

focused prayer for diaspora peoples. An armchair approach to prayer is not enough. Prayer is needed in the morning, short prayers before each meal, and entreating God on behalf of diaspora peoples when we wake up and before we go to bed. At the same time, we need our prayers laser focused for specific people groups among whom Christ is largely unknown.

Movements of people groups toward Christ come when Christians are on their knees. Not only must we center our strategies around Jesus Christ as the pivotal truth for all of humankind's problems and rely upon the Holy Spirit's convincing power, but we must pray. We must pray for them by the diaspora people group's name. We must pray that God will intervene into the problems of their lives.

The Bible speaks of our responsibility to know, discover, and be intentional about engaging diaspora peoples residing among us, no matter whether they are new immigrants, refugees, or international students.

Leviticus 19:34 says,

> The foreigner who resides with you shall be to you as the citizen among you; you shall love the foreigner as yourself. (ESV)

Acts 17:26-27 says,

> And he made from one man every nation of mankind to live on all the face of the earth, having determined allotted periods and the boundaries of their dwelling place, that they should seek God, and perhaps feel their way toward him and find him. (ESV)

A majority percentage of diaspora peoples have never heard the truth of the gospel in a way that they can understand or make sense from their worldview perspective. These unreached[5] peoples are our neighbors.

We need the whole body of Christ praying, connecting, embracing them and reaching them with the love and truth of the Gospel of Jesus Christ and then be available to disciple them in their context.

WE NEED TO BREAK OUR ROUTINE
TAKING TIME NATURALLY
ENCOUNTERING THEM, BECOMING
THEIR FRIENDS, HEARING THEIR LIFE
STORIES, AND AT THE SAME TIME
MINISTERING TO THEM BOTH IN WORD
AND DEED.

When it comes to what churches do with diaspora peoples, sometimes it is like rearranging deck chairs on the Titanic. Somebody has to patch up the leaky boat. Are Christians adding their autobiography to God's historical redemptive record by discovering, encountering, and engaging diaspora?

The sovereign God who is orchestrating the migrations of peoples is calling the body of Christ to reach diaspora peoples for his glory. God entreats us to join him in his historical plan of salvation for all diaspora. Like a child being

---

[5] A people group is considered "unreached" when Christ is largely unknown and the church is relatively insufficient to make Christ known in its broader population without outside help.

picked for a team, we stand before God raising our hands saying, "pick me!" What an opportunity that God is providing us so we eagerly embrace the task of reaching the nations.

This brings us to a model that will guide us in reaching the nations and diaspora people ...

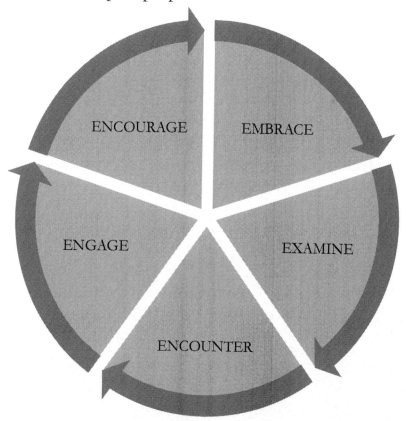

The above model is a hands-on approach to learn from God's Word plus to discover, encounter, engage, minister to and disciple diaspora peoples. Each of the five above are disciplines we must develop for reaching the nations. We develop each one as we repeat them over and over. No single one is more important than the other. The five disciplines will help you gain knowledge and experience to ...

- Eagerly embrace God's heart for diaspora peoples.
- Carefully examine who are the diaspora peoples in your locale and where do they hang out.
- Naturally encounter diaspora peoples to form lasting relationships.
- Intentionally engage and minister to the needs of diaspora peoples.
- Mutually encourage one another that results in learning from new diaspora disciples and also discipling them in their context.

In addition, when implemented in a local metro area, the disciplines will provide handles that ...

- Voice God's passion for all peoples and especially those who are dispersed throughout the world for one reason or another.
- Motivate us to join God in reaching the nations.
- Discover specific people groups that exist in a locale.
- Unearth unreached and unengaged people groups.
- Help you to learn where and among whom to emphasize your evangelistic efforts.
- Break down the task of engaging diaspora peoples.
- Equip you in practical ways to begin a conversation with diaspora people and discipling new converts.
- Keep you from focusing personnel and resources on people and places that are less strategic.
- Provide a framework for relating with diaspora peoples as co-laborers.

This book guides you to reflect, pray, and respond to each of the five disciplines as you consider how God is calling you to serve among diaspora peoples. You will interact and write down responses to various sub-topics as you work through each discipline. In addition, after working through each discipline, you will answer, "What is God teaching you about this Discipline?"

Others [6] have written on various subjects of diaspora peoples. In fact, the use of 'diaspora' has proliferated in the past two and a half decades. Just over 20 years ago, discussions of ethnicity and immigration paid little attention to diaspora (Safran 1991, 83). Could it be that the topic is now discussed more wide-spread because previously diaspora people coming to North America originated mostly from European with Christian worldviews whereas in the past 20 years plus they have originated from many other parts of the world and therefore we recognize the differences more readily?

This book does not claim to be exhaustive concerning every subject matter about diaspora. However, this does not negate the importance of this book.

We are often unaware of the various diaspora peoples within arm's reach. God is calling Christians, no matter whether we serve in a professional minister role or not. What a privilege and opportunity God sets before us. What a time in history when we can walk out of our houses and meet people who otherwise would never have the opportunity to hear the

---

[6] A noteworthy author on diaspora is Enoch Wan. See his publication entitled Diaspora Missiology: Theory, Methodology, and Practice.

message of Christ. A colleague often reminds me that God not only invites us to get on the plane but also to meet those who arrive on plane in our locale.

Since diaspora peoples are still connected back to their family and friends in their homeland, reaching them makes sense practically and missiologically. Diaspora people, once reached, have the greatest potential to reach back to their homeland seeing their family, friends, and their own distinct people group come to Christ.

The subtitle of this book is "People that Change the World". At first glance, we might assume it refers to diaspora peoples. Obviously, they are changing the world and nations where they reside.

However, what if the subtitle referred to all Christians? What if all Christians took on the mantle to reach the diaspora.

I remember the day very clearly when I heard God ask me, "Whom shall I send, and who will go for us?" (Isaiah 6:8). Similar to a student in the classroom who knows the answer that a teacher asks, I quickly raised my hand and said to Jesus Christ, "Here am I, send me."

GOD ENTREATS US TO JOIN HIM IN HIS
HISTORICAL PLAN OF SALVATION FOR
ALL DIASPORA.

With the above in mind, this book's target audience is the church and specifically followers of Christ who are now interested in answering the question, "Who is my neighbor?"

DISCIPLINE 1
EMBRACE
"GOD'S HEART FOR DIASPORA PEOPLES"

As emphasized in the introduction, the peoples of the world are stepping into our living room in what seems to be a permanent move. Millions of people around the globe are on the move. Migration has been a human reality throughout history. Diaspora peoples come with different backgrounds, worldviews, and dispositions toward life.

The waves of diaspora peoples is an unfinished story. Even though governments say they plan to reduce the numbers, the advancements in travel and telecommunications along with a number of other factors point to more, not less, in the years ahead. This growing wave and their responsiveness should demand increasing attention. Despite this, many Christians often overlook and are silent about the significant unreached bloc of diaspora peoples.

THE BIBLE IS NOT SILENT
CONCERNING MIGRATIONS AND
DIASPORA.

The Bible paints a picture that the nations and diaspora are important. In fact, the Bible itself is a story of migration; an exodus of generations.

This discipline looks at what the Bible says about migrations, diaspora peoples, and people groups. It begins looking at the table of nations and Abraham's call. Next, it will delineate Biblical passages that reveal God's heart for the nations and propose that God is orchestrating the movements of peoples. Last, it will recommend a cross-cultural response to migrations is needed requiring us to relook at how we so often interpret Acts 1:8.

The Table of Nations

The lengthy genealogy list, known as the Table of Nations, beginning in Genesis 10 and continuing through Genesis 11 provides a background of world history in understanding the origin of "people groups" and the phenomenon of migrations. The original unity of the peoples of the world is represented by the view that all the nations originated from Noah's sons (See Gen. 9:19). As time passed, the various families were separated by language and land, with the birth of divergent cultures (Gen. 10:5, 20, 31). The scattering of the families stimulated the emergence of various people groups, each with their own common affinity of language, culture, and etc. The Bible views the scattering and emergence of the various people groups of the world as the Lord's judgment upon people for their sin of self-assertion (Gen. 11:4). Thus, "the Lord scattered (the peoples) abroad from there over the face of the earth" and "confused the language of all the earth" (Gen. 11:8-9).

The Call of Abraham

It is interesting that following the Table of Nations we come to Genesis 12. Not without purpose, Gen. 12 follows Gen. 10-11, the origin of people groups. God did not abandon people. Instead, he called Abram to shine forth as a blessing for all the peoples of the world (Gen. 12:1-3).

INTENTIONALLY ENGAGING PEOPLE GROUPS REFLECTS THE VERY CHARACTER AND NATURE OF GOD.

From the beginning of time to the present, God continually seeks to initiate reconciliation between himself and his fallen creation. For instance, when Adam and Eve acquiesced to Satan's temptations in the Garden of Eden, God came searching for them, calling, "Where are you?" (Gen. 3:9) And again, when humankind fell into a state of utter wickedness (Gen. 6:1- 5, 11-12), God sought out Noah to replenish the earth and made a covenant with Noah (Gen. 6:18-22). All of these activities point to the fact that God is a God of Grace.

Now, with Abraham, God saw the scattering and emergence of the various people groups and sought out someone, a man from Ur, to become a messenger of hope and peace for all people (Gen. 12:1-3). The promise of universal blessing to the nations of the earth is repeated in Genesis 18:18; 22:18; 26:4; 28:14. So the blessing of Abraham is intended by God to reach out to diaspora peoples mentioned in Genesis 9-11.

God's Heart for the Nations

God intended that his people would be the instrument for diaspora. This theme of God's intent that all people groups know Him is seen throughout the Bible.

- Exodus 19:6 -- Israel was to be a "kingdom of priests"

- Deuteronomy 4:6-8 -- show your understanding to the nations
- Deuteronomy 10:19 -- "You are to love those who are aliens"
- Joshua 4:24 -- "so that all the peoples of the earth might know"
- 1 Samuel 17:46 -- "the whole world will know there is a God in Israel"
- 2 Kings 19:15 -- "Hezekiah prayed . . . : O LORD, you alone are God over all the kingdoms of the earth.'"
- 1 Chronicles 16:31 "Let the earth be glad; let them say among the nations, The Lord reigns!'"
- 1 Chronicles 16:24 -- "Declare his glory among the nations, his marvelous deeds among all peoples"
- 2 Chronicles 6:33 -- "so that all the peoples of the earth may know your name and fear you"
- Psalm 2:7-10 -- "You are my Son . . . I will make the nations your inheritance"
- Psalm 18:49 -- "I will praise you among the nations"
- Psalm 22:26-28 -- "all the families of the nations will bow down"
- Psalm 45:17 -- "The nations will praise you for ever and ever"
- Psalm 46:10 -- "I will be exalted among the nations"
- Psalm 47 -- "God reigns over the nations"
- Psalm 66 -- "All the earth bows down to you . . . Praise our God, O peoples"
- Psalm 67 -- "your salvation among all peoples"
- Psalm 72 -- "all nations will serve him"
- Psalm 72:17, 19 -- "All nations will be blessed through him . . . May the whole earth be filled with his glory"
- Psalm 82 -- "all the nations are your inheritance"

- Psalm 86:8-13 -- all nations will come and worship
- Psalm 99:1-3 -- "He is exalted over all the nations. Let them praise your great and awesome name"
- Psalm 105:1 -- "make known among the nations what He has done"
- Psalm 117 -- "Praise the Lord, all you nations"
- Psalm 126 -- "it was said among the nations"
- Isaiah 42:6 -- "I will keep you and will make you to be a covenant for the people and a light for the Gentiles."
- Isaiah 37:16 -- "O Lord Almighty . . . , you alone are God over all the kingdoms of the earth."
- Isaiah 49:1-6 -- "I will make you a light for the Gentiles"
- Isaiah 56:7 -- "my house shall be called a house of prayer for all nations"
- Isaiah 60:3 -- "Nations will come to your light"
- Isaiah 66:19 -- "They will proclaim my glory among the nations"
- Jeremiah 16:19 To you the nations will come from the ends of the earth and say, "Our fathers possessed nothing but false gods, worthless idols that did them no good."
- Ezekiel 36:22-23 -- "The nations will know I am the Lord"
- Daniel 7:13, 14 -- "all peoples, nations and languages should serve Him"
- Jonah's story -- the missionary book of the Old Testament
- Micah 4:2 -- "Many nations will come"
- Zephaniah 2:11 -- "Nations on every shore will worship him"
- Haggai 2:7 -- "Desire of all nations"

- Zechariah 2:11 -- "Many nations will be joined with the Lord in that day and will become my people"
- Zechariah 9:10 -- "He will proclaim peace to the nations"
- Malachi 1:10-11 -- "My name will be great among the nations, from the rising to the setting of the sun"
- Matthew 24:14 -- the gospel will be preached in the whole world
- Matthew 28:19-20; Mark 16:15 - The Great Commission
- Mark 13:10 -- "the gospel must first be preached to all nations"
- Luke 2:32 -- "a light for revelation to the Gentiles"
- Luke 10:2 -- "harvest is plentiful, but the workers are few"
- Luke 10:27 -- "love your neighbor as yourself"
- John 3:16
- Acts 1:8; 2:5-12 13:47 (Isaiah 49:6) -- witnesses in all the earth
- Acts 3:25 -- He said to Abraham, "through your offspring, all peoples on earth will be blessed."
- Acts 13:47 -- "I have made you a light for the Gentiles, that you may bring salvation to the ends of the earth." (Isaiah 49:6)
- Romans 1:5 -- "We received grace and apostleship to call people from among all the Gentiles to obedience."
- Romans 3:29 -- "Is God the God of Jews only? Is he not the God of Gentiles too? Yes, of Gentiles too."
- Romans 15:10 "Rejoice, O Gentiles, with his people." (Deuteronomy 32:43)
- Romans 16:26 -- So that all nations might believe
- 2 Corinthians 10:16 -- "so that we can preach the gospel to the regions beyond you"

- Galatians 3:8 -- "The Scripture foresaw that God would justify the Gentiles by faith, and announced the gospel in advance to Abraham: All nations will be blessed through you.'" (Genesis 12:3; 18:18; 22:18)
- Galatians 3:14 -- "He redeemed us in order that the blessing given to Abraham might come to the Gentiles."
- Ephesians 2:11-19 -- "you are no longer foreigners and aliens"
- Hebrews 6:13-14 -- God's promise to Abraham
- Revelation 5:9 -- "you purchased men for God from every tribe and language and people and nation"
- Revelation 7:9 -- Every tribe, tongue, people and nation
- Revelation 14:6 -- "The angel had the eternal gospel to proclaim to those who live on the earth -- to every nation, tribe, language and people."
- Revelation 15:4 -- "all nations will come and worship before you"
- Revelation 21:23-24 -- "The Lamb is its lamp. The nations will walk by its light"

 Look over the above scripture passages again and reflect upon what God is teaching.

The Divine Maestro

God uses war, persecutions, educational desires and needs, and economics all for the advancement of his redemptive history. The Bible is very clear that God "desires all people to be saved and to come to the knowledge of the truth" (1 Timothy 2:4) no matter where they rest their head.

THE MIGRATION OF PEOPLES IS MORE THAN A SOCIOLOGICAL PHENOMENON.

It is intertwined into God's sovereign plan for humankind. God is moving people so that those who are least reached can freely encounter the gospel of Jesus Christ. As JD Payne states,

> God is at work through the mass movements of peoples from the rural communities to the cities, from fleeing persecution, war, and starvation to lands of security and prosperity, and from departing areas where educational and economic lift are rare to locations where such matters are assumed to be the norm. (2012)

While on Mars Hill, the apostle Paul spoke about God's plan. Luke records Paul's words saying,

> And he made from one man every nation of mankind to live on all the face of the earth, having determined allotted periods and the boundaries of their dwelling place, that they should seek God, in the hope that they might feel their way toward him and find him. Yet he is actually not far from each one of us (Acts 17:26-27, ESV).

God is sovereign and he is the divine maestro orchestrating the movement and migrations of peoples. God's heart desires diaspora peoples of the world find and know Jesus as their Lord and Savior.

Cross-Cultural Response for Diaspora Peoples

Since the time of Abraham until the end of the age the call of God's people is to make disciples of people from all nations and people groups. Acts 1:8 says,

> But you will receive power when the Holy Spirit has come upon you, and you will be my witnesses in Jerusalem and in all Judea and Samaria, and to the end of the earth. (Acts 1:8, ESV).

One way to view Acts 1:8 is from a geographical perspective. In other words, we begin as witnesses in our Jerusalem, then move onto Judea, then to Samaria and ultimately to the end of the earth. From a geographical perspective, we might say that we serve first as witnesses in our metro area or city and then move to the state or province then expand to our own country and ultimately to different countries.

Another way to look at Acts 1:8 is from a socio-cultural-linguistic perspective. In so doing, we serve as witnesses first to our family and friends (our oikos), then to people of the same socio-cultural-linguistic makeup as we are, then move onto people who have a similar socio-cultural-linguistic background and finally to people who are completely different socio-culturally-linguistically.

Both the geographical and socio-cultural-linguistic perspectives have merit. However, we are faced with a dilemna in metro areas due to the migration of people and the transient nature of peoples in the world.

DIASPORA PEOPLE ARE NOT
GEOGRAPHICALLY DISTANT FROM US.
ON THE OTHER HAND, WE ARE OFTEN
SOCIALLY DISCONNECTED FROM THEM
AND ARE CULTURALLY AND
LINGUISTICALLY DIFFERENT FROM
THEM.

The catch is that though they often reside in close proximity to us their social networks and the people that they often eat with, hang out with, and even worship with are not the same as ours.

Making it even more challenging is the fact that what they feel comfortable with socially, culturally, and linguistically is often not what we feel comfortable with. In Discipline 3, we will look more in depth how culture subtly trains us, restricting our lifestyle to those with whom we so often find comfort in our day to day lifestyle.

When we see missions strictly as going to a geographical place, then we often miss God given mission opportunities to the people we pass by everyday.

The socio-cultural-linguistic implications from Acts 1:8 include becoming cross-cultural and extending our social networks to peoples who are different socio-cultural-linguistically. As such, it points to the need for entering the space of people who we normally have no association.

Just like God who became flesh and dwelt among us (John 1:14), we too should incarnate the Word of God among diaspora.

When we cross cultures and enter the spaces of people who are different than us, God provides us the opportunity to extend His Kingdom by forming a lasting relationship that leads to ministering to their needs and discipling them as Christians. These are topics that we will visit in Disciplines 3-5.

Use the following to list how you are involved from a geographical perspective of obeying Acts 1:8. Also, list some ways that you can improve.

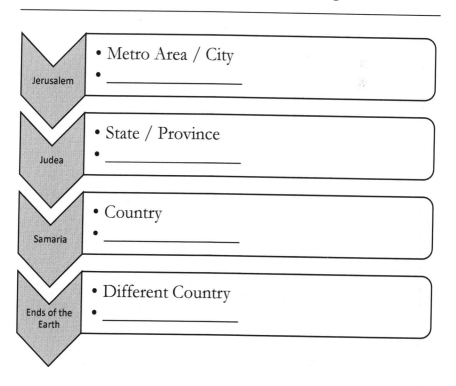

Jerusalem
- Metro Area / City
- _____

Judea
- State / Province
- _____

Samaria
- Country
- _____

Ends of the Earth
- Different Country
- _____

Use the following to list how you are involved from a socio-cultural-linguistic perspective of obeying Acts 1:8. Also list some ways that you can improve.

Jerusalem
- Family and Friends
- _____

Judea
- Same Socio-Cultural-Linguistic
- _____

Samaria
- Similar Socio-Cultural-Linguistic
- _____

End of the Earth
- Different Socio-Cultural-Linguistic
- _____

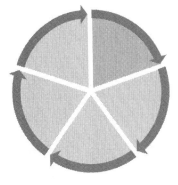

WHAT IS GOD TEACHING YOU ABOUT THIS DISCIPLINE?

EMBRACE
God's Heart for the Nations

DISCIPLINE 2
EXAMINE
"WHO AND WHERE"

Discipline 1 ended with our examining our existing relationships to fulfil our roles as witnesses in Jerusalem, Judea, Samaria, and the end of the earth. We evaluated our witness both from a geographical and socio-cultural-linguistic perspective.

Now it is time for us to go more in depth, expanding our sphere of social networks and places where we do everyday life. In so doing, we will find bridges to connect with diaspora. Said another way, we carefully examine our surroundings to discover where diaspora peoples reside, do everyday life, and socialize with one another.

Examine surfaces signposts to the existence of people groups within a specific locale. It carefully seeks to answer two basic questions: who is here and where do they hang out.

IF WE, THE CHURCH AND CHRISTIANS,
ARE RESPONSIBLE TO REACH DIASPORA
PEOPLES, WHICH WE ARE, THEN WE
MUST BE INFORMED.

We must know our surroundings so well that we know what nations have come near us, what languages they speak, etc. Passion that is misinformed often results in misunderstanding. We have a passion to communicate a message. We should never let this passion depart. However, if the message is not communicated properly, it becomes misunderstood and even rejected for the wrong reasons. Conversely, when we take time to gather information, we can avoid such miscommunication traps.

Who is Here?

To answer this question, we can turn to census data, demographic, religious, consulate, immigrant, refugee, and educational sources. This data is often public information that can be unearthed by anyone. However, every context is different and the availability and depth varies from place to place and from country to country.

Such public information often unearths and paints a picture of the broader ethnic makeup, nationalities, ancestral heritages, and languages spoken at home within a country or locale. In some contexts, such information is not always readily available to the general public and must be purchased via the government or another agency.

 List data sources that inform who is here. Who has that information and where is that information available (cite specific source)?

 From your listed data sources or from personal experience, begin making a list of nationalities and languages spoken in your locale.

If known, list the specific people group names with their population, general locations, and their status toward evangelical Christianity (unreached [7], no longer unreached, etc.) along with their engagement status (unengaged with no intentional church planting strategy underway, engaged with an intentional church planting strategy underway).

Where do they hang out?

Discovering where specific diaspora people groups socialize with one another and hang out begins with finding Points of Interest (POI). Points of Interest (POIs) are geographical locations where one may encounter clusters of people groups or specific people groups. In other words, POIs are places where diaspora people groups gather, hang out, and socialize in some way with one another.

Points of Interests (POIs) are natural bridges to encounter and engage people. A few POIs types include:

Ethnic Business
Ethnic Restaurant
Islamic Mosque
Other Sacred Point of Interest
Shinto Shrine
Hindu Temple
Jain Temple

---

[7] A people group is considered "unreached" when Christ is largely unknown and the church is relatively insufficient to make Christ known in its broader population without outside help.

Buddhist Temple
Consulate / Embassy
Ethnic Association
Ethnic Market / Grocery
Jewish Synagogue
Refugee Agency
Ethnic School / Institution
Sikh Gurdwara
Housing Community / Apartment Complex
Park / Recreational Place

The above list of POI types serves as a beginning point. Every context is different. Therefore, there are no strict guidelines on what POI types are best for discovering diaspora peoples in your locale.

It is theologically and missiologically sound to meet diaspora peoples on their turf. A missionary once came to the field to do sports evangelism. He was going to conduct sports camps. When asked how will the people know about the camps, he thought for a moment and did not reply. His missionary colleague then asked him, "why not go where they play sports and meet some of them?" He further added, "Why not form a relationship with them having a sports camp right where they play the sport and leave them in the places that they are most comfortable?"

POINTS OF INTEREST (POI) ARE
NATURAL BRIDGES FOR
ENCOUNTERING DIASPORA PEOPLES.

They are the places where they feel most comfortable and at home. Moreover, people are more open to us when we enter their spaces than they are when they are a minority in our spaces.

 Read John 4:1-4

John records that Jesus "had to pass" (John 4:4) through Samaria. It would be easy to assume that this phrase implies a geographical reference. However, the route Jesus took was purposeful as it was not the only route between the two provinces — in fact, it was not the most common one.

From Galilee, Hebrews would travel east and cross over the Jordan river in order to bypass going through Samaria. This was all because of their ethnic prejudices toward Samaritans. Prejudices were so deep that Hebrews equated Samaria with a foreign country and not a part of the Holy Land.

Some scholars view this "had to pass" language as referring to a "compulsion other than mere convenience. As the Savior of all men, Jesus had to confront the smoldering suspicion and enmity between Jew and Samaritan by ministering to his enemies" (Tenney 1981, 54).

Jesus did not hesitate traveling through Samaria, all the while looking for a point of interest where he could encounter Samaritans, those to whom his culture had taught him to avoid. In essence, Jesus understood that divisions between people groups are not merely geographical in nature but are much deeper, at the level of social and cultural.

Just as Jesus, we are to cross into new territory where diaspora peoples are and purposefully go to those points of interest (POIs) that we tend to hesitate or make us feel uncomfortable. We will continue looking at John 4 in the next four Disciplines.

 What Points of Interest types are in your locale? What places of worship other than Christian can you find? Etc.??? Which POIs types would you hesitate encountering?

 Make a list of specific Points of Interests (POIs) in your locale.

 WHAT IS GOD TEACHING YOU ABOUT THIS DISCIPLINE?

EXAMINE

Who is here and Where do they hang out?

DISCIPLINE 3
ENCOUNTER
"FORM LASTING RELATIONSHIPS"

You have begun unearthing Points of Interests (POIs). Remember these are possible hangouts for immigrants, refugees, international students. You also sifted through public data that serves as possible signposts for the existence of people groups in your locale. You have also begun listing diaspora people groups, that possibly exist within your locale.

It is now time to naturally encounter diaspora people groups and verify their existence. Encounter seeks to discover the specific people groups who reside within specific locales. The purpose of encountering people groups at places where they hang out is to form lasting relationships with people that sees them come to faith in Christ, discipled, and emerge as leaders among their people group.

 Read John 4:5-9

How did the Samaritan woman know that Jesus was a Jew? Was it how Jesus spoke? Was it the way he dressed? Was it how he was sitting? Did Jesus smell like a Jew?

There was a line of demarcation between Jews and Samaritans. The text says, "For Jews do not associate with Samaritans." (John 4:9)

Jesus grew up in Jewish culture. He was socio-culturally and linguistically clothed in Jewish culture. He dressed as a Jew would dress. He spoke with a Jewish accent[8]. He ate what Jews ate. He even smelled like a Jew.

His culture also taught hatred between Jews and Samaritans. This hatred was fierce and long-standing. In some ways, it dated all the way back to the days of the patriarchs.

Culture is dynamic and powerful. It teaches us how to perceive the world and our surroundings. It teaches us what ...
... food we should eat.
... clothing we should wear.
... homes we should build and live in.
... transportation we should use.
... roads we should travel.
... songs and music we like.
... holidays we will celebrate.
... ways we earn a living.
... language we will consider our mother-tongue.

Culture also teaches us how to ...
... act and behave around people from our own culture.

---

[8] It is generally agreed by historians that Jesus and his disciples primarily spoke Aramaic (Jewish Palestinian Aramaic), the common language of Judea in the first century AD, most likely a Galilean dialect distinguishable from that of Jerusalem. See Matt. 26:73 where Peter was warming his hands by a fire in the courtyard.

… cook the food we eat.

… drive a car.

… greet others and be polite.

… bury the dead.

… make decisions and choose leaders.

… rear and discipline children.

… etc.

CULTURE TEACHES US HOW TO SEE,
PROCESS, AND INTERPRET OUR
CULTURAL SURROUNDINGS.

As an example, how many colors do you see when you see a rainbow? Most Americans maintain that there are seven colors in a rainbow. Traditional Japanese perceive six colors by seeing blue and green as one color. Another people in the world perceive four colors by seeing light, dark, wet, and dry colors. There actually are thousands of colors in a rainbow. Culture constrains people to see a rainbow differently.

 How do you see the world? Take time to reflect how each of the following influence your perspective of the world.

- What do you do with your free time?
- How do you view roles in your family?
- What type of home do you live in?
- How do you greet others?
- What are your three most important values in life?

Culture fashions our mental map of objective reality, answering what is important and how to act and behave.

CULTURE SHAPES OUR CULTURAL
PREFERENCES, OUR LIKES AND
DISLIKES, HOW TO SEE THE WORLD
AND WHO BELONGS IN OUR WORLD
AND WHO DOES NOT.

Jesus was clothed culturally as a Jew. The Samaritan woman for some reason recognized that Jesus was a Jew. She wondered why this Jew would associate and even speak to her. The Jewish cultural preference that Jesus had learned taught do not associate with Samaritans.

<u>Jesus saw beyond his own cultural preferences</u>. (John 4:7)
    A woman from Samaria came to draw water. "Give me a drink," Jesus said to her.

Jesus' Jewish cultural preferences taught him to not associate with Samaritans. Moreover, it taught him to not speak to Samaritan women. Nevertheless, Jesus saw beyond his own cultural preferences. If we are not careful in cross-cultural encounters, our cultural preferences can offend others.

I often remind myself, "offend people for the right reason not the wrong reason." The right reason is the power of the cross. The wrong reason is imposing my cultural preferences upon diaspora which could include ...

*   Curling up and not relating to certain types of people groups just because I am uncomfortable.

- Not accepting hospitality from diaspora (e.g. eating food offered us that we think is strange, etc.)
- Greeting someone according to how I was taught yet not realizing that every people has different ways of greeting one another. (e.g. shaking hands, a hung, etc.)

CULTURE INDOCTRINATES INSOFAR
THAT IT BLINDS US TO OTHER WAYS OF
BEHAVING.

Our actions and motivations will seldom conflict with those of the group in which we were raised. We learn our culture so well and abide by it that we do not realize there are other ways of doing things. For instance, greetings vary from shaking hands, bowing, nodding, etc. These ways of doing things become subtle everyday habits of what we deem as appropriate behavior.

A few others include gestures, ways of sitting and standing, tone of one's voice, loudness and/or softness of one's voice, ways of eating (with fork, spoon, chopsticks, hands, etc.), what hand to eat with (right or left hand), ways of asking directions (indirect or direct), ways of walking, etc. Such a list is a book in its own right.

Look back over what culture teaches us (See pages 30-31). List things that your culture teaches you. Reflect for a moment upon the question, "what cultural preferences tell me to not engage diaspora and certain types of diaspora people groups?"

<u>Jesus also saw beyond his own cultural prejudices</u>. (John 4:9) "How is it that you, a Jew, ask for a drink from me, a Samaritan woman?" she asked. For Jews do no associate with Samaritans.

The Jewish culture not only said "do not associate with Samaritans" but also, "do not speak to a woman."

The Jewish cultural preference to not associate with Samaritans led to cultural prejudices. If we are not careful, our cultural prejudices can blind us from seeing people's needs. Discipline 4 will look at ministering to needs.

 Take time to reflect upon any cultural preferences you have learned that could lead to cultural prejudices.

The worldview perspective which Jesus learned as a Jew was to not associate or speak with Samaritan. However, Jesus did not let his worldview perspective keep him from engaging a people other than his own, the Samaritan woman.

Understand the Differences in Worldview Perspectives

Interwoven in the urban crowds are a kaleidoscope of people groups. They are diverse socio-culturally, economically, ethnically, and linguistically, all seeing their environment through their worldview perspective and all with distinct values of their own. One no longer need travel outside one's own country to encounter a diversity of worldviews. In fact, differing worldview perspectives are now as close as next door.

<u>What is worldview?</u> While visiting a small island between Okinawa, Japan and Taiwan named Irabu-jima, I was asked an interesting question. A priest for one of the indigenous religions asked, "What island are you from?" As the conversation continued, it was discovered that the priest had never traveled to any other place except for the few small islands near his home island. Basically, he viewed the world as being made up of islands. As a result, from his worldview perspective, the question seemed natural. The priest's geo-political background influenced him to see the world from a specific perspective. He grew up on an island, had only traveled to a few other islands, and therefore, viewed the world from the perspective of being made up of islands.

The norms that shape how people see the world come from a variety of norms: which include: (1) geo-political, (2) socio-cultural, (3) religious, (4) ethnicity, and (5) linguistic.

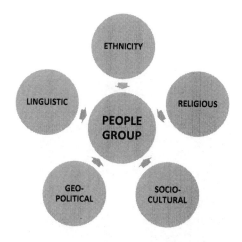

Norms that Shape Who People Are

The combination of these norms or influences shape how a person will see the world, or their worldview.

The term worldview comes from the German translation of Weltanschauung. Weltanschauung is defined as "a comprehensive conception or apprehension of the world especially from a specific standpoint." (Merriam-Webster Dictionary). As A.F.C. Wallace (1970) states:

> [A worldview is] the very skeleton of concrete cognitive assumptions on which the flesh of customary behavior is hung.

Accordingly, he continues, the worldview of an individual ...

> may be expressed, more or less systematically, in cosmology, philosophy, ethics, religious ritual, scientific belief, and so on, but it is implicit in almost every act.

In short, worldview is a person's overall perspective or lenses for understanding and interpreting life. It is a person's basic assumptions of their world, providing a coherent mental and emotional map for making sense of one's surrounding. It is expressed in the what one deems important in life (their value system) and seen through their behavior and the ways they interact with other people.

A person's cultural background and upbringing shapes a person's worldview. Exposure to different cultural practices or mores, or changes in geography or living circumstance, or significant tragedy or success — such experiences shape one's way of thinking about life and meaning. Such experiences determine one's worldview.

A gap between worldview perspectives often exists in cross-cultural encounters, resulting in miscommunication or misunderstanding. The concept of worldview is foreign to many, if not all of us. Therefore, let's begin by illustrating where worldview comes.

<u>Worldview Illustrated</u>. People go through life using their worldview constructs absorbed from childhood. Throughout Asia Pacific, these constructs often come from religious rituals and rites, which all the while inform worldview. For instance, on Irabu-jima, the people's worldview is shrouded with animism and shamanism. Accordingly, they see the world being inhabited by myriads of spirits. As such, for the people on Irabu-jima, these constructs give shape to how they relate to one another, outsiders, and the world in which they live. They, like clockwork, constantly ask the spirits for good favor. When they don't ask, they create disharmony, resulting in a poor harvest and economic success.

The people of Irabu-jima perform their religious rites and rituals asking the spirits for a good harvest. These rituals and rites not only thanked but also entreated the spirits for a good harvest. Having a long history, these rituals and rites are performed before and after a harvest. According to tradition, the spirits may be communicated with through the agency of the "yuta," whose role is performed almost exclusively by women. The yuta is an intermediary between the spirit world and those of the village. The world that can't be seen is closely intertwined with the world of the living (Negishi, Mayumi 2000:PG). The yuta has supernatural power to see, hear and discern the cause of misfortune and advise action to be taken. These "yuta" women are consulted for ill health, dream analysis, suitability of marriage partner, matters related to the tomb, selection of a house site, economic hardships, and even politics. The yuta and her practices are deeply rooted in the social structure as one is able to see the role of women in having economic success.

Shamanism is popular and well-patronized in Irabu-jima while at the same the people reside in one of the world's most developed nations. Needless to say, the people of Irabu-jima, as is the case throughout the majority of Okinawan prefecture, move comfortably between modernism and shamanism for treatment and counsel (Allen 2002). When it comes to working among such a people, one should realize that religious rituals and rites inform how the people act and behave, how they make decisions, what they see as acceptable and unacceptable, and what they value and deem important. In other settings, other cultural phenomena may inform worldview. Nevertheless, the values and assumptions people hold concerning the world often lead to fixed views of others, all which makes up their worldview.

The majority of the dispersed people groups are no different than those who reside on Irabu-jima. Many go to shamans for counsel. Many people, even those who are affluent and living in the context of modernism, still perform daily rituals and rites to maintain social harmony with the spirit and sacred world. Their worldview perspective forces them to adhere to specific assumptions, premises, and practices.

Worldview Universals. All people hold assumptions and premises concerning the world. As previously mentioned, these assumptions and values come from five different norms: (1) geo-political, (2) socio-cultural, (3) religious, (4) ethnicity, and (5) linguistic. People group formation occurs as some norms become more dominant than others in shaping one's worldview.

As an example, the western business worldview is driven by a rational economically free market society. Moreover, it is most often English language oriented. Such cultural dynamics drive the assumption that anyone can succeed economically in life if he or she only tries hard enough. Such influences give rise to valuing individualism, or the self and one's personal convictions being most valued. Therefore, the dominant norm that shapes worldview is socio-cultural.

On the other hand, many people view economic success resting in the hands of the spirit world. They, in turn, delicately strive to maintain harmony with the spirit world, resulting in performing certain rites and rituals on a regular basis. Such influences give rise to valuing collectivism, or the group and loyalty being most valued. Hence, the dominant norm that shapes worldview is religious.

Often there are fine lines between the dominant norms that shape people group formation. Nevertheless, through naturally encountering people groups, one can discover the norms that are dominant in shaping a people's worldview. As a result, one will learn the basic assumptions and premises of the people group, helping to close the gap for good communication to take place as two different worldviews meet.

People also categorize cultural phenomena. Most people recognize and categorize the family unit. However, how they group families together is often different dependent upon their cultures. Some people group family in terms of extended family groups or think in terms of clans, while others are more exclusive. Such categorization determines how people view self. For some people, self-identity rests in how others see them, while in other settings it comes from how they see themselves. Moreover, for some people, self-identity rests in how they view themselves in relation to the group. In other words, they first ask, "What is good for the group?" Whereas, for others, especially those coming from an American culture, they first ask, "What is good for me?"

As another example, people categorize time, space, and cause and effect. Some people process time linearly while other people process time circularly. In terms of how people view space, when people come from different cultures that have different expressions of personal space, relationships between them can be uncomfortable. People also have different views on the cause and effect of events in their life or how to produce change. As is the case in Irabu-jima, the people view the cause of poor economics stemming from being out of harmony with the spirit world and not receiving good favors. Other people, though, might view the cause more naturally (e.g. dry weather, infertile soil, etc.).

Cross-Cultural Implications

A gap in worldview perspectives exists in cross-cultural encounters. To bridge this gap, it is needful to follow several guidelines as we naturally encounter people groups.

Be sensitive and vulnerable. Go as a learner. Being a learner begins with eating the same food that the other people eat or following protocols on entering, sustaining, and exiting conversations. Observing local customs can often stretch one beyond personal comfort zones. Nevertheless, such steps in sensitivity and vulnerability are needed if one expects to close the gap between worldview perspectives. When it comes to another people's local customs, we need to remind ourselves that our way is not always the best way – it is just one way.

Learn about their context. Closing the gap also comes from studying the cross-cultural context, looking beneath the surface and asking specific questions concerning worldview. For instance, as Gesteland (2002) asks, "are the people we are encountering more deal focused or more relationship focused?" Deal-focused people, such as Americans, ten to immediately get to the point in discussions. They immediately get to the point. On the other hand, relationship focused people, such as most Asians and South Americans, build and work through relationships. They, consequently, often follow certain cultural protocols before talking about certain things. A few other questions to ask would include:

- How are group or individual decisions made?
- Do the people come from a more informal or formal culture?
- Do the people view time as rigid or fluid?
- Are the people more expressive or reserved in their behavior?

Enlist cultural informants. Invite the people to tell you the "should" and "should nots" in their culture. Give these cultural informants permission to inform, correct, and modify how you speak and behave. In doing so, informants can provide valuable insider information on the deeper aspects of culture and help prevent you from breaking cultural protocols that harm relationships and widen the gap between worldviews. These cultural informants often become the lifeline of closing the gap.

<u>Conform to their way of doing and saying things</u>. Paying attention to one's surrounding and the people in that surrounding is often a good way to learn how one should act, behave, and even what to say. Once observed, test the observation by mimicking such behavior and ways of speaking. By testing, you can begin to discover if what you are doing is appropriate. However, at this point, it is always appropriate to refer to your cultural informant.

<u>Lead with Love</u>. Often when people know we care about them, they forgive our mistakes.

What worldview perspective do the people groups near you have? Are you sensitive and vulnerable to their worldview? Have you taken time to learn their worldview and enlist cultural informants? Do you strive to conform to their way of doing things?

 In what ways should you conform more to their way of doing and saying things?

Closing the gap between worldview perspectives helps one avoid misunderstanding and even more important miscommunication. The time and steps are a worthwhile investment.

 Using your initial list of people groups ... begin reading articles, profiles, etc. on them to better understand their worldview.

Making Changes in Our Patterns in Life

We can easily create patterns in life that often keep us from the very places where people groups hang out in our locale. Or, we go to those places and then never intentionally bring missions close to home.

Culture often tricks us, due to subtle changes around us. As such, we often become so familiar with our surroundings, that we miss the neighbors, markets, salons, etc. that have moved into our communities. Even when we notice the presence of new people and places we often treat them as strangers doing our business as usual.

 Make a list of patterns in your life that you can tweak so that you will more intentionally encounter people groups in your locale. As an example, buy your fresh fruits and vegetables at an ethnic supermarket.

A Model to Naturally Encounter

We may ask, "I am at a Point of Interest (POI), so how do I begin a conversation?"

<u>Utilize the 5-W Question Words</u>. The 5-W Question Words consist of Who, What, Where, When, and Why. Using these five question words can unearth a wealth of information from people. These 5-Ws help avoid asking closed ended questions and precipitate a flow of conversation with open ended questions.

<u>Focus on 5-F Subject Words</u>. The 5-F Subject Words center around: Family, Friends, Food, Festivals, and Future.

5-F	5-W
FAMILY	WHO
FRIENDS	WHAT
FOOD	WHERE
FESTIVALS	WHEN
FUTURE	WHY

Combined with the 5-W Question Words (Who, What, Where, When, Why) mentioned previously, the 5-Fs can unearth almost anything about a people and their culture. As a simple illustration, one could ask:

- Who is in your family?
- What does your family do?
- Where does your family live?
- When does your family get together?
- Why does your family get together?

The 5-Fs above do not stand alone in themselves. For instance, family questions would include issues related to husband-wife, siblings, age appropriateness, gender issues, etc. Friends would also include seeing who the people view as enemies or those that they do not deem as their friends.

A simple memory approach for asking questions is place the 5-W Question Words on one hand with each finger representing one of the 5-W Question Words and then do the same for the 5-F Subject Words. In so doing, one need not be concerned with memorizing an exhaustive list of subject categories or questions that one could ask.

 Take time now and use the 5-Fs and 5-Ws to find out about someone.

Immersing Yourself at Points of Interest

There are no absolutes regarding immersing yourself at Points of Interests (POIs). Nevertheless, several general guidelines do exist.

Encounter People Groups in Natural Everyday Settings. Immersing ourselves should not be a sideline activity. Instead, it should be part of everyday life. Every day we see and have an opportunity to meet people, and every one of these encounters serves as a way for understanding a people. Hence, immersion should be a part of everything we do.

A few ways to begin immersing yourself among people groups include:

- Visit Sacred, Religious sites (e.g. Buddhist temple, Islamic mosque, etc.)
- Eat at ethnic restaurants (e.g. Malaysian restaurant, Thai restaurant, Vietnamese restaurant, etc.)
- Shop at ethnic supermarkets
- Attend ethnic festivals
- Go to places that they work

In short, immersing yourself is done by visiting the places that people groups in your locale reside, work, worship, and associate with one another.

TAKE NOTE: Critical in the immersing process is making objective observations and asking culturally sensitive questions. Without both, one can easily draw conclusions that are not true concerning people.

<u>Be a Regular</u>. Frequent the same places where people groups gather. Attending once is not enough. Productive encounters take time which involves going back to the same places. Therefore, spend quality time at your points of interest … moreover frequently going to a specific POI builds trust by allowing the people to become familiar with who you are.

<u>Watch People in Context</u>. By observing people in context, an incredibly rich understanding of what the people really need will surface. Sometimes it is more important to take one's time and just watch what others do, how they do it, and only then ask them to explain what something means.

God sends us into the world to listen and to connect, which means sometimes we can learn by watching. We do well to remember Saint Francis' instructions to his monks, "Preach the Gospel, use words if necessary, what we say matters."

<u>Ask Culturally Appropriate Questions</u>. Badly phrased questions produce misleading results. Avoid closed-ended questions which encourage the answer "yes" or "no."

<u>Talk to the Right People</u>. Talking to people at a railway station, for example, will get answers from commuters; but

if one wants information on people who stay at home with young children, then it is needful to talk to those people where they gather. Moreover, opinion leaders often provide invaluable information but so do followers of opinion leaders, especially if they are spoken to in separate venues.

Talk to Enough People. Talking to two people, for example, won't provide enough objective information. Each person talked to will give a different perspective, or piece of the puzzle, about their people group. It's important to talk to a wide sampling of people (both men and women) from different socio-economic groups, age groups, occupations, etc. The more discussions, the clearer the overall picture of your people group will be.

Keep Each Encounter Impartial. It's easy to encourage people to give the answer desired. For example, by asking leading questions or smiling at the "right" answer one can induce answers that the people think you want to hear.

Interpret Results with Care. Drawing the right conclusions from immersions is extremely important. Bear in mind that people encountered may distort answers based on what they think you want to hear.

Be Realistic. It can be tempting to pick out that which confirms what you want to hear, and ignore the rest. By ignoring the rest, you can damage how you design your strategy. Be prepared, no matter how out of line with what you want to hear, to modify information and your plans based upon what the people are saying.

Focus upon the Person not a Task. Naturally encountering diaspora peoples is not a project. The end goal is being relational and involved in the lives of diaspora peoples. In short, be vulnerable and open your life to them.

Narrowing Down Your Options

You have discovered many POIs, are seeking to see beyond your own cultural preferences, beginning to understand the people's worldview, made changes to your patterns in life, utilizing the 5-Fs and 5-Ws to form initial relationships, and are immersing yourself at various Points of Interests.   As you continue this journey, you are beginning to discover that every Point of Interest (POI) is not necessarily a Point of Engagement (POE). Therefore, it is time to begin narrowing down your options and where you spend your time and among whom.

Be careful and don't quickly make a judgment that a POI is not a POE.   Sometimes it might be the time you visit the place. It also could be you are speaking to the wrong person at the place. Or, it might be some other reason.

Nevertheless, as you frequent Points of Interest (POIs), time will come when you will need to narrow down your options and the places that you visit.

THIS NARROWING DOWN IS A
SPIRITUAL JOURNEY YOU WILL FACE.

It requires much prayer.   It also requires a discerning spirit and heart.

In the story of Jesus and the Samaritan woman, why did Jesus sit down by the well?   There were other places that he could have encountered people. He could have sat down along the road and encountered people as they walked by.

Had he been watching people come and go from the well? Had others already visited the well before Jesus spoke to the Samaritan woman?

Whatever the case, Jesus met the Samaritan woman at a Point of Interest (POI) that he discerned as a Point of Engagement (POE).

Several characteristics exist for discerning whether a POI is a POE. Obviously, a POE is a place where people groups hang out. Second, a POE is a place where one can naturally encounter people who are friendly and also willing to have a conversation.

A POE IS A SPECIAL KIND OF PLACE
WHERE CONVERSATIONS CENTER
AROUND THEIR LIFE STORIES AND
VICE VERSA SHARE YOUR LIFE STORIES.

To begin narrowing down your options of POIs to POEs, consider the following questions ...

- How many times have you visited the POI?
- Have you visited at different times of the day or days of the week?
- Have you spoken with different people?
- Have you heard their life stories?
- Have you prayed enough to make a decision?

Look over your list of Points of Interest from Discipline 2 and begin narrowing down your options and where you will focus your time and energy.

WHAT IS GOD TEACHING YOU ABOUT THIS DISCIPLINE?

ENCOUNTER

"Form Lasting Relationships"

DISCIPLINE 4
ENGAGE
"MINISTER TO DIASPORA PEOPLES"

Encounter is not an end in itself. It serves as a bridge to intentionally engage diaspora peoples. Mentioned in Discipline 3, we need to be vulnerable. Vulnerability happens when we open our lives up to diaspora peoples, sharing with them the difference Christ has made in our lives as followers of Jesus.

In other words, we use our own life story of how faith in Jesus Christ ministered (served) to a need in our own life.

 Read John 4:10-26

How did Jesus treat the woman at the well? First, as the great bridge builder, he asked for a drink. This was the beginning of an interesting conversation.

Christ assumed a posture of humility by asking her for help before he helped her. Following a brief discussion about living water, Jesus put His finger on both the need and problem area of her life. Without judging her in any way He told her that He knew she was living with a man who wasn't her husband and that she had already had five husbands.

Jesus knew this woman's deepest need – her need for acceptance – and when He met it she believed in Him and automatically became a most enthusiastic witness – and probably laid the foundations for the later revival in Samaria (Acts 8).

As another example, Zacchaeus had a need for friendship. Jesus met his need by going to his home to offer the real friendship and fellowship that a home visit and social meal implies.

So, similar to Jesus, we can begin ministering to a diaspora people's needs the first time we encounter them. For instance, before having a meal in an ethnic restaurant we can ask the waiter or waitress the following, "We are Christians (followers of Jesus) and we say a prayer before we eat thanking God for what he has done and is doing in our lives. What needs do you have that we can voice in our prayer?"

Learn about and Begin Meeting their Needs

Every culture and all people face deep and personal needs – a few include:

- Loneliness
- Managing relationships
- Family and parenting
- Handling money
- Finding fulfillment
- Coping with stress and worry
- Workplace problems
- Safety needs from war and persecution.
- Physical needs brought on by natural disasters, famine, etc.

- Facing illness
- Honor

The above list could continue. Needs are the result of the fall of man which created separation between God and mankind. We often call this separation and this self-centered nature, the total depravity of humankind. As a result, needs exist in every culture and among every people. In this sense, needs are the unescapable rites of passage of humans.

Moreover, how sin manifests itself socially and culturally is different in every culture and among every people. As a result, different needs surface in each cultural context.

People specific needs are precisely the amplifier that God very often uses to begin a process that ends in conversion. Of course, God is sovereign throughout this process. But it helps us to understand this progression – and the 'Gray Matrix' is a remarkable insight into God's plan.

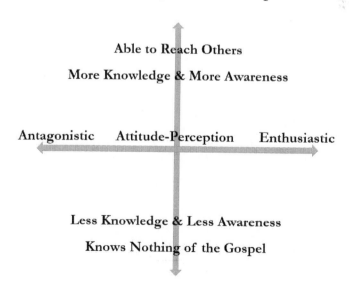

Taking time to understand the knowledge-awareness level of a people concerning the gospel message is invaluable. Such understanding is needed. However, as Gray's Scale indicates, effective communication of the gospel also entails understanding a people's attitude-perception of Christianity.

Needs are linked to both knowledge-awareness and attitude-perceptions levels. In other words, as people move from levels of no knowledge-awareness to more knowledge-awareness and from being antagonistic to enthusiastic toward the gospel, not only do their needs change but they also move to new levels of receptivity.

When we understand the methods that God uses to speak to people at different levels on this scale, we can work with God to communicate the Gospel appropriately and contextually to meet a people's needs.

NEEDS ARE A BRIDGE TO THE PEOPLE,
A STEP ON THE ROAD OF LEADING A
PEOPLE TOWARD CHRIST.

Probably one of the most important aspects of engaging people groups is ministering (serving) to their needs, no matter whether that need be a physical, cultural, social, or spiritual need. Ask God to give you a discerning and sensitive heart for diaspora peoples and their specific needs.

If the people group comes from a refugee background use ministries that promote community and belonging like sports, reading clubs, sewing clubs, etc.

If the people group does not speak English, use ESL classes to serve them and share truth. Use Bible stories to teach conversational English.

Theravada Buddhists recognize a higher power (nirvana). One of the reasons Theravada Buddhists want to achieve this void of nirvana is because of its permanence. They view it as a secure destination to hope for amidst the chaos of daily life. Hence, the permanence Theravada Buddhists hope for in nirvana points to deeper life issues and needs among Theravada Buddhists.

Hindus believe that actions are ruled by the Law of Karma. They can do things which are judged as wrong. They identify those actions as wrong and bad consequences in his life, both now and in future existences, because of certain actions. Hence, the consequences of actions point to a need among Hindus.

All peoples everywhere have needs. As we naturally encounter people, forming lasting relationships with them, we at the same time should intentionally engage them ministering to and serving their needs.

Formulate Hunches to Identify Needs

With the above in mind, how does one go about identifying needs among a people and within a culture? Asked another way, how does one formulate "hunches" concerning problems that exist among a people and within a culture?

<u>Share Needs in Your Own or Another Culture</u>. This sort of sharing is not threatening if it initially focuses upon the predicament of an outside community.

Informal settings are the most appropriate for this approach of identifying needs. Even if one works with another culture, it is possible to find parallel needs from one's own culture or other people and cultures.

Ask How They Deal with Death, Birth, Sin, Initiation Rites. As the previous approach, informal settings are the most appropriate for this approach. Such topics can be asked as one goes about doing everyday life activities.

Use Bridges to Discover and Meet their Needs. Jesus took an everyday activity, drawing water from the well, and turned it into a bridge to minister to the woman about living water.

JESUS USED A (HIS OWN) PHYSICAL
NEED TO BRING SPIRITUAL TRUTH.

Buddhists believe in reincarnation. Use their concept and need of wanting to be born again, which means reincarnation in their worldview perspective, to explain rebirth in Christ. Ask them when their birthday is. After they respond, then say you have two birthdays. You can share concerning your physical (when you were born and where) and spiritual birth (your testimony).

Write and Talk to People with a Similar Culture. These are peoples and cultures with close cultural affinities to the people and culture. Close cultural affinity might come in the form of language, customs, and beliefs.

Share a Written Need of a Similar People. These often serve as catalysts for identifying needs. For example, it is possible to tell a life story to people and then ask them how they would respond to the situation.

If they do not respond or the life issue does not apparently seem to bother them, then it is quite possible that the particular need does not exist among the people. On the other hand, if they relate the story to their own lived experiences, then it is quite possible that the need exists among the people.

Share Bible Stories that Answer Questions of Needs. Once the Bible story is told, ask people how they would respond to the situation.

Please Note: present the situation as dramatically as possible. Many immigrants and refugees come from cultures of great story-tellers who listen attentively to a well told story. Remember that extensive introductions make a boring story, besides one does not have the time to tell a long story in this form of inquiry. Remember to keep the story short, asking people almost immediately how they would respond or what truth the story teaches.

Answering Some Questions. Are the people experiencing rapid culture change? Have the people recently or are they presently experiencing natural disasters, war, etc.? When people have recently or are presently experiencing such situations then a people begin questioning their traditional values, norms, and beliefs. In such circumstances, several needs surface (e.g. safety, security, etc.).

To summarize possible approaches to discover needs, remember to go as a learner expecting a *kairos*[9] moment. Some useful questions for knowing whether the particular issue is really a need among the people include: "How would you see the problem?" "Why is there a problem?" Their answers to these questions will let you know if you have presented the need well and if the need exists among the people.

Do not ask them if they have the same problem among their people. Such a question is closed-ended and people will often respond according to what they think the questioner wants to hear and not necessarily how they really feel about a particular issue.

Use holidays for bridge building. As an example, at Christmas when people say "happy holidays", ask them which holiday they are celebrating. They actually might be celebrating a religious festival other than Christmas.

Begin plotting where on Gray's Matrix (see page 53) the people are, then list needs (your hunches) about the people being encountered. Last, relate each need to a Bible story, then memorize the Bible story to share with a person.

---

[9] Kairos (καιρός) is a Greek word meaning the right, critical or opportune moment.

Don't Get Side-tracked

Jesus did not get side-tracked in the conversation when the Samaritan woman asked, "Why is it you a Jew ask me for a drink?" (John 4:9)

Jesus basically ignored the question, which was actually a confrontation type of question because of the division and hostility between Jews and Samaritans, men and women.

Then another time the Samaritan woman sought to side-track the conversation. The Samaritan woman said to Jesus, "Our fathers worshiped on this mountain, yet you Jews say that the place to worship is in Jerusalem." (John 4:20) Jesus again just moved on and did not get side-tracked.

When we encounter people, we might not agree with many things they say or they might even be confrontational (e.g. During conversations with Muslims, they will often interject in a conversation that the Bible is corrupted). When this happens, don't get side-tracked and instead stay focused on listening well for their needs.

> THERE IS A TIME AND PLACE THAT YOU SHOULD ADDRESS ISSUES, ARGUMENTS, WRONG PERCEPTIONS, ETC. THAT THEY HAVE CONCERNING CHRISTIANITY AND THE CHURCH.

However, the point here is as you encounter and begin engaging diaspora don't get side-tracked to the point that you miss an opportunity or even close their heart's door to future conversations.

Pray for Diaspora Peoples Needs

Ministry to diaspora peoples begins and ends with prayer both corporately and individually. Before encountering and engaging pray. While encountering and engaging pray. After encountering and engaging pray.

PRAYER-WALK AS YOU ENTER A POINT OF INTEREST ASKING GOD TO OPEN DOORS AND GUIDE YOU TO THE RIGHT PEOPLE.

Always be ready to offer a prayer for them and their needs. I personally have never seen diaspora reject an offer to pray for them when they are asked about their needs. Always end your prayer in the name of Jesus. Guide them to pray to Jesus for their needs.

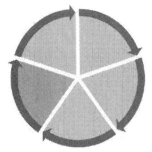

WHAT IS GOD TEACHING YOU ABOUT THIS DISCIPLINE?

ENGAGE
"Minister to Diaspora Peoples"

DISCIPLINE 5
ENCOURAGE
"DISCIPLE DIASPORA PEOPLE IN THEIR CONTEXT"

Our journey began when we first asked ourselves, "who is my neighbor?" Since then, we have discovered who our new neighbors are, formed a friendship with them, heard their life stories during mealtimes and other occasions. We have also ministered to their needs.

Our process began with meeting diaspora peoples at the places (POIs) where they find comfort socially, culturally, and even linguistically. As we frequented those POIs, we discovered some were places (POEs) where we could begin sharing life with one another. One more step is needed, a step of seeing them embrace Christ as their Savior. This step asks us to answer, "who is the person of peace (POP) among this dispersed people?" Once discovered, we partner together in our journey of faith in Christ. We both, in turn, mutually encourage one another as servants of Christ.

 Read John 4:39-42

Jesus met the Samaritan woman's need of acceptance. She then accepted the message of Jesus Christ, and in turn introduced this man Jesus into her sphere of social networks by telling others of her experience with Jesus Christ. She became a bridge into the lives of others.

In fact, the Scripture says, "the Samaritans came to him [Jesus Christ], and asked him to stay with them." She spoke so highly of Christ and created so much interest among other Samaritans that they took the initiative to welcome Jesus into their home. Jesus stayed with them in Samaria for two days (John 4:40).

This implies that Jesus lived with the Samaritans, stayed and ate with them to teach and disciple them. Jesus was invited and welcomed into their context. He did not seek to extract them from their context, requiring them physically to come to his social, cultural and/or religious context.

Leave Them in Their Context

It is interesting that Jesus did not require them to meet him on his turf. Instead, he willingly accepted their hospitality resting his head in a new place and also eating with them no matter what they served.

So often, when we discover someone like the Samaritans who are receptive to the message of Christ, we extract them from their existing networks and invite them into our own networks. This is often true in how we do church.

> ONCE A SIGN OF RECEPTIVITY APPEARS
> AMONG A PERSON OR DIASPORA
> PEOPLE, WE SHOULD ALL THE MORE
> LEAVE THEM IN THEIR CONTEXT.

Most Hindus, Buddhists and Muslims will not feel at home in our churches. Those who seek and are open to hear the truth of the gospel will need to be led to Christ and discipled in their context.

Immigrants, refugees, and international students often follow other major world religions (e.g. Hinduism, Islam, Buddhism) or a minority religion (e.g. Zoroastrianism, Jainism, and Sikhism). There are places of worship for all of them. Many African people groups also follow their traditional ethnic religions.

Most diaspora people from other faiths feel better worshipping in their own places of worship, eating food at their ethnic restaurants, and socializing with others like themselves in culturally familiar contexts.

LEAVING THEM IN THEIR CONTEXT ALLOWS THEM TO REMAIN CONNECTED WITH THEIR *OIKOS*[10], THE PEOPLE WITH WHOM THEY HAVE THE MOST INFLUENCE.

Extraction and attraction models do more harm than good in reaching a person's sphere of social networks.

As soon as someone shows interest in the Gospel, offer to start a Bible study in their context, preferably in a neutral place. Minister to and disciple those open to the gospel in small groups in neutral settings such as a house, local coffee

---

[10] Oikos is a Greek term for "family and household". It means much more than one's biological family or household and includes a person's web of social networks with whom they regularly socialize.

shop, park, etc. Leave them in their natural environment and do not extract them from their specific group context.

 Read John 4:27-30

We again turn to John 4 to learn from the story of the Samaritan woman. John 4:27-30 teaches a few ways in which we can deal with an issue that might rise up along the way and also ideas for discovering a Person of Peace.

Before the woman began spreading the news of Christ, the other disciples arrived and questioned within their minds, "why is our teacher speaking with a Samaritan and especially with a woman who has questionable morals?" (my paraphrase). Yet none of the disciples voiced publicly any opposition or astonishment.

How did John know the disciples were astonished? Was John himself among the disciples who had such a reaction? Had the disciples discussed or murmured among one another what they were thinking? Or, was it the way they looked at one another that signaled their amazement?

For some reason, they were struck speechless by their shock and when that wore off, Jesus was already teaching them about His mission. Jesus was teaching them to see beyond their own cultural preferences and prejudices. He was teaching them that all people are included in God's sovereign plan. Jesus stayed the course even in the midst of his own disciples questioning where all of this was heading.

Stay the Course

Possibly at this stage in your journey other Christian friends have joined you in engaging diaspora peoples. Some may have questions about who you are engaging or the approach you are using. Whatever the case, stay the course, and stay focused, staying within their context and leaving them in that context.

Even as they remain in their social, cultural, and linguistic context, the question begs us, "how do I discover and recognize if someone is a Person of Peace (POP)?" In other words, at the POEs and with the people to whom I have formed a relationship, how do I probe to see if he or she is a Person of Peace (POP)?

Ways to Discover and Recognize POPs

The concept of People of Peace is a popular topic. Many people have discussed and written about the topic. Some provide prescriptive lists based upon Luke 10. In a real sense, such lists can give one the impression that if followed one will be led to people of peace. Such a prescriptive list approach appears lacking theologically, missiologically, and practically speaking.

It is like making a list of ways to predict how, where and among whom God is going to work. God is sovereign and is the Redeemer. We are just his instruments on this journey of sharing how Christ has brought us to Himself.

With the above in mind, the following ways for discovering and recognizing people of peace do not claim to be an exhaustive list. Moreover, the following list is not prescriptive nor is it predictive but is just what I have learned as I have lived out God's Word among diaspora. In addition, it should be noted that the following ways are not necessarily dependent upon one another.

Ask Questions Rather Than Make Pronouncements. Read John 4:28-30. The Samaritan woman spoke to the people, who actually had no respect for her, by phrasing her discovery of the Messiah in the form of a question. Her question (in Greek) implies a negative answer: "This is not the Christ, is it?" If she had stated boldly that she had met the Christ, they more than likely all would have laughed and returned to their conversation. But her question, framed as a tentative suggestion, piqued their curiosity.

As you form relationships, frame your teachings of Jesus Christ in the form of questions. Let them draw their own conclusions of who Christ is. This approach also will assist in discovering who among the people is a Person of Peace (POP). A few questions may include ...

- What spiritual beliefs do you have?
- To you, who is Jesus?
- Why do you think Christianity is (true, false, just another religion, etc.)?
- What happens after you die? Where does one go after they die?
- What is this story telling us about God? (after telling a Bible story).
- What benefits does following the teaching of Christ make in one's life? (After sharing your personal testimony or sharing someone's testimony.)

- What makes a person good? How does a person become good?

On the other hand, pronouncements are leading and not necessarily good ways of seeing if people are interested in Christ. Open-ended questions serve as means for probing whether a person is possibly a Person of Peace.

Welcomes Conversations about the Messiah. The Scripture (John 4:28-29) says that the woman left her water jar and told others that "someone treated me with respect, accepted me, knew my need, and is possibly the Christ, the Messiah for all peoples, even us Samaritans" (my paraphrase).

As Samaritans, close cousins to the Jews, they also expected a Messiah, one who would accept and welcome them for who they were, despite all their blemishes.

All of a sudden, at that moment when the woman began thinking that Christ was the Messiah, she moved from being not just a Point of Engagement (POE) but a Person of Peace (POP).

A PERSON WHO WAS MORE THAN
INTRIGUED ABOUT CHRIST BUT WAS
ALSO WILLING TO RECEIVE CHRIST AS
HER TEACHER FOR LIFE.

People of Peace not only share their life stories and hear yours, but also welcome conversations concerning Jesus Christ. Said another way, they want to learn about Jesus. They are not just intrigued but want to learn about Jesus on their own and want Jesus to become their teacher concerning life.

In a practical sense, they are willing and want to read the Bible. Hence, one way to discover whether someone is a Person of Peace is by asking them to read the Bible and then letting them know that next time you get together you will ask them what they have learned. The Gospel of John is one among several good Scripture texts to have them begin reading.

<u>Curious about Spiritual Issues</u>. Apparently all 70 disciples found people of peace (Luke 10:17). God is sovereign leading us to people of peace when the time is right.

Being sovereign, God is working in the hearts and minds of people. For instance, God was already at work in the life of Cornelius (Acts 10: 1-2, 22). The Bible called him a God-fearer. God fearers were non-Jewish people who tried to keep the Law of Moses. They were righteous people who sought answers in life.

Curiosity is sometimes a sign of people who are searching for truth and answers in life.

CURIOSITY AND RECEPTIVITY WORK
HAND IN HAND.

Discipline 4 considered how as people move from less knowledge to more knowledge, and also from less antagonism to being more enthusiastic they become more receptive to the Gospel and teachings of Christ. What is happening is they are becoming increasingly curious about finding answers in life.

One way I use to probe the area of curiosity is via asking their interests. What they have often wondered about in life? What is the meaning of life? Etc.?

Responds Positively toward a Gospel Presentation. Read Acts 10:44-48. Ultimately, when culturally understood, a person of peace will receive the gospel and believe. The key here is culturally understanding the gospel. I think one of the biggest reasons why we often miss discovering people of peace is because our communicated Gospel message is not in a form that makes sense within their worldview perspective.

To test the waters of understanding of the gospel presentation, as they read Scripture ask them questions. Providing an exegetical interpretation of the Scripture for them is not always necessary.

> GOD WILL WORK IN THEIR MIND AND HEART TO INTERPRET SCRIPTURE BASED ON THEIR SOCIO-CULTURAL-LINGUISTIC WORLDVIEW PERSPECTIVE.

For instance, I was telling a Bible story and asked, "who in the Bible story was the most important?" The person I picked out in the Bible story as being the most important was completely different from the person they picked. I was seeing the text via my cultural lenses and they were doing the same. God is in control and will act in their lives and spirit in a dynamic way. Let God's Word work.

<u>Willing to Follow Christ's teachings no matter the risks</u>. People of peace seem to respond whole-heartedly to Christ. They love Him more than family or possessions or status, once they've come to know Him. A POP examines the demands of the cross and is willing to lay down his or her life.

 List the names of people that you have encountered at Points of Engagement (POEs) who appear to have the marks of a Person of Peace (POP).

Begin Discipling the Discovered POP

The following are some overarching ways to begin discipling someone who you believe is a Person of Peace.

<u>In the context of their relationships</u>. Promote *oikos* (home) evangelism: guide them to share what they are learning and to share with others within their network. Tell them that just like they heard the message of Christ from you, they too should share the same message with their family and friends. Also, encourage them to have their oikos present when you disciple them in the Word. In this way, you birth a home church not a convert.

<u>Encourage them to share their testimony</u>. The Samaritan woman returned to town and shared her testimony (John 4:39). She did not wait until she knew everything about following Christ. Instead, she immediately told the people in her circle of relationships what had happened.

A personal testimony is powerful because it is about one's self and not someone else. People may not believe after hearing the Gospel but they can never disclaim a personal testimony.

THE FOCUS OF A PERSONAL TESTIMONY SHOULD CENTER AROUND JESUS. THE FOCUS IS ABOUT WHO JESUS IS AND WHAT WE HAVE PERSONALLY "SEEN AND "HEARD" IN REGARD TO WHO HE IS.

Our faith in Christ story is for everyone and not just a specific audience. It should illicit a response of "wow, God is so amazing in sending Jesus to rescue us. I want to hear more about this Jesus." This is the reason the Bible calls the gospel "good news".

With this in mind, coach the person of peace to frame their testimony in their own words sharing that testimony in words that make sense according to their own socio-cultural-linguistic context. Remember that both you and the person of peace are on the journey together. Therefore, therefore this time should be the most fun journey one has ever had whereby you both are mutually encouraged.

Invest in them, don't move around. (Luke 10:7) Once you find a person of peace, concentrate on them. Don't spread your witness so thin that you don't invest in them properly. Remember, they are 1) the key to a network of folks, 2) the avenue through which a new church will gain credibility in the community. It also gives them a true friend. Most people accept Christ because you have become their friend and they believe the credibility of your life.

Accept them as they are. (Luke 10:8 "eat what is set before you"). You must come to them on their terms. Spend time with them, eat with them and don't refuse anything they offer.

Let them minister to you also. (Luke 10.7-8) As previously mentioned, be vulnerable sharing your struggles but at the same time share how you deal with your struggles because of your new life in Christ.

MUTUALLY ENCOURAGING ONE ANOTHER BY BEING VULNERABLE AND SHARING STRUGGLES AND VICTORIES TEACHES FROM START THE NATURE OF FELLOWSHIP.

By letting them take responsibility for you, you allow them to reap a blessing and teach them the importance of doing the same with others that they will encounter and also share a message of hope through Christ.

Help them count the cost beforehand. Jesus makes it clear to those who follow Him what it was going to cost. If you want the POP and his oikos to really be strong, growing disciples and for the new church to be bold and not timid, they must understand what it will cost beforehand.

Use Bible Storying. Bible stories are easier to remember and they promote faith. Most of the following key teachings can be illustrated/taught with Bible stories.

- The Father who knows and loves us
- Jesus our main leader
- The Holy Spirit our main teacher
- The power and authority of the Word of God, the Bible
- The reality of spiritual warfare and our authority in Christ

<u>Give them a vision for Church</u> – Give the POP a vision that goes beyond personal conversion, and includes their whole oikos. Rather than scaring them away from their oikos, it includes their oikos and speaks to their heart.

In other words, do not just make a convert but also plant a home church. There is much joy in seeing those who have not heard and who did not have access to the gospel in their homeland come together to worship Jesus Christ.

The above practical ways to disciple diaspora are not exhaustive of all that we need to do to disciple and raise up leaders.

 List other practical steps you can take to disciple a person of peace.

WHAT IS GOD TEACHING YOU
ABOUT THIS DISCIPLINE?

ENCOURAGE
Disciple Diaspora People in their
Context

NEXT STEPS

The five disciplines are a repeating process of embracing to encouraging. Wherever you are in your journey of reaching the nations, you will have a next step, whether that be embrace, examine, encounter, engage, or encourage. In other words, as disciplines, we never reach a point where we have perfected any one discipline nor do we want to get stuck on one discipline. We always strive at being better doing all five disciplines.

Each time I approach God's Word I learn something new and grow more in my understanding of a God who loves all peoples, no matter who they are. In the same way, every time I begin forming relationships with diaspora peoples, God teaches me something new.

 Read John 4:31-38

This passage is filled with several truths for taking next steps in reaching diaspora peoples.

God Supplies All We Need (John 4:31-34)

While the Samaritan woman went into town, the disciples returned from town having purchased food. However, Jesus no longer felt physical fatigue as his hunger had disappeared. Instead, he emphatically says, "I am refreshed by nourishment hidden from you. I have food that you do not know about."

The disciples somewhat bewildered assume someone had already brought him food. They questioned among themselves, "Has anyone brought him something to eat?" So, here Jesus is to their amazement. His hunger is gone, exhaustion has ended, and he has a fresh vigor from their journey through Samaria. How could this be? Jesus replies that he obeys the "will of him who sent me and to accomplish his work."

Jesus was sent to meet the needs of all people, and in this case a Samaritan woman. By doing the will of the Father, all of Jesus' physical needs were met.

Jesus was teaching the disciples that ultimately in life God is the supplier of all our needs and in following his will all of our needs will be met.

 What has God already provided (e.g. people, resources, etc.) for you in reaching diaspora peoples?

Harvest Force Issues (John 4:35)

The disciples thought it was not time to harvest. They said, "There are yet four months, then comes the harvest." The disciples were hesitant to enter the fields because they could not see the possibilities of a present harvest.

JESUS WAS TEACHING HIS DISCIPLES TO
LOOK BEYOND THE NATURAL TO THE
SPIRITUAL HARVEST.

He was teaching his disciples that the problem was not with the harvest field, it was a problem with the harvest force.

 What are some of the reasons why we and others, the harvest force, are hesitant to go in the harvest field of diaspora peoples?

 What can we do to help ourselves and others, the harvest force, overcome hesitancies for reaching diaspora peoples?

The Fields are Ready for Harvest (John 4:35)

Jesus continues saying, "look, I tell you, lift up your eyes, and see that the fields are white for harvest." Jesus desires that the disciples see the fields as he sees the fields, white for harvest. Jesus addresses the possibilities that exist within the harvest field.

 What present possibilities exist within your locale that point to the fact that the fields are ready for harvest?

People Play Various Roles (John 4:36-37)

Jesus says, "One sows and another reaps." Jesus refers to himself as the sower and the disciples as the reapers. In a field, it was not uncommon that some planted the seeds while others harvested the goods. The time of the harvest is always a time of joy. So, naturally, the harvester often receives the praise. Yet, interdependency was necessary for the harvest to occur.

Jesus was teaching the disciples that some serve as sowers and others serve as reapers. But more, both roles were equally important, as both the sower and reaper can rejoice together.

The truth learned is each one of us play a different yet equally important role in engaging diaspora peoples. All of us approach the task in humility because God invited us to join Him.

Comparing it to a race, we carry the baton part of the way, as far as God allows us, then we trust the Spirit has another runner who will carry the baton.

 What role does God want you to play in reaching diaspora peoples in your locale?

Others Have Labored (John 4:38)

Last, Jesus says, "I sent you to reap that for which you did not labor. Others have labored, and you have entered into their labor." Jesus gives reference to the Old Testament laborers (e.g. the prophets) and John the Baptist. All of those laborers cultivated the soil, planted seed, etc.

Who do you know, can speak to, and learn from who has labored among a diaspora people? If you are able to contact them, then send them a note, an email, or phone them, thanking them for service in God's Kingdom of Reaching the Nations.

Concluding Remarks

Whether we for the first time are reaching the nations or we have been reaching people groups for years, each one of us have a unique next step to take as we grow in our faith journey with Jesus and diaspora peoples. We, though, firmly know that in the end, there will be ...

a great multitude that no one could number, from every nation, from all tribes and peoples and languages, standing before the throne and before the Lamb, clothed in white robes, with palm branches in their hands, and crying out with a loud voice, "Salvation belongs to our God who sits on the throne, and to the Lamb!" (Revelation 7:9-10)

Five Disciplines for Reaching the Nations

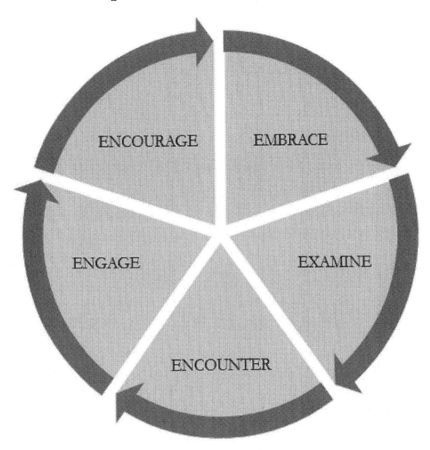

APPENDIX

Challenges from Within

When people migrate, two divergent cultures clash bringing challenges. The greater challenges come from within our own lives as our socio-cultural-linguistic background clashes with the diaspora peoples socio-cultural-linguistic background. But reaching them can bring life to us – a renewed missionary vision and vigor. Nevertheless, a few challenges we might face include ...

<u>Finding balance in ministering to needs (social mandate) and proclaiming the Gospel (evangelistic mandate)</u>. Diaspora peoples are sometimes inundated with physical, social and spiritual needs. We, in turn, could become consumed with only ministering to their physical and social needs and never addressing their spiritual need.

The Bible stresses making disciples of all peoples while at the same time caring for one's neighbor by feeding the poor, clothing the naked, and visiting the prisoner (Matthew 25:35-45). Finding balance between the evangelistic mandate and the social mandate of the Gospel should not be a challenge.

However, it becomes a challenge when we minister to physical and social needs first then at another point in time will address the spiritual need. In so doing, we dichotomize life into the secular and the sacred. Sociologically, a large percentage of peoples in the world integrate all aspects of life and do not compartmentalize life in various departments. When we compartmentalize life into the sacred (spiritual need) and secular (physical and social needs), we get stuck. Instead we should find balance ministering to needs while at the same time proclaiming the gospel.

When we dichotomize the social and evangelistic mandates, we also open the door to misunderstanding and distortions of the gospel among peoples that do not dichotomize life. Practically, ministering to the entire person and the collective community provides a connecting point for transporting the Gospel message.

Communicating with diaspora peoples. Misunderstandings are common among people who speak the same language, so it's not surprising that people from different cultural and linguistic backgrounds face communication barriers. Anything from the mispronunciation of a word to a lack of specificity can lead to misunderstandings.

Communication goes beyond spoken language. Cultural differences in body language and other behaviors can also cause miscommunications. For example, in the United States, it is important to make eye contact with someone who is speaking to you or they may think you are distracted or uninterested. However, in many Asian countries, eye contact can be a sign of disrespect or a challenge to authority.

There are many other cultural differences in body language that can create barriers to effective communication. Those include differences in facial expressions, the use of nodding to indicate agreement or understanding, and the amount of space to give someone with whom you are having a conversation. The communication challenge can and often does cause miscommunication of the gospel message, which leads to the next challenge.

<u>Contextualizing the Gospel Message</u>. The gospel is best understood when it is communicated in a person's heart language. Moreover, the gospel is best understood when it is clothed in cultural forms that are familiar to the person (e.g. music in worship, etc.).

<u>Ethnocentrism</u>. Ethnocentrism is focusing only on the needs of yourself and your own ethnic origin, believing that you are the center of the universe. All people have some degrees of ethnocentrism in their attitude and concept toward others. Missiologist Eugene Nida states,

> In considering the relationships between people and cultures, we tend to regard ourselves as the only ones who make judgments - or at least accurate ones. We must not forget for a moment that other people make judgments of us, and that some of them are not too complimentary (1954:7).

A survey of scripture shows that ethnocentrism has always plagued mankind thinking what one's own culture does is right and/or superior and what other cultures do is wrong and/or inferior.

For instance, in Joseph's day Egyptians did not eat with Hebrews because such table fellowship was "detestable to Egyptians" (Gen. 43:32). Agrarian Egyptians also considered shepherds "detestable" (Gen. 43:34). In the New Testament, we see Jews and their ethnocentrism toward the Samaritans.

Ethnocentrism begins with preconceived ideas of someone else. We arrive with preconceptions concerning the diaspora people. On the other hand, the diaspora people also have preconceptions of our role, our identity, and our faith. These pre-conceived ideas can be both negative and positive.

Value challenges. A clash of cultures also means a clash of cultural values. The most successful anthropological and missionary methods of approach to non-Christian peoples have resulted not from theoretical formulations dreamed up in the isolation of one's study but from on-the-spot dealing with the complex, living situations.

Fully equipped with our own sets of values, of which we are largely unconscious, we sally forth in the world and automatically see behavior with glasses colored by our own experience. Nowhere is this automatic behavior revealed more striking than in the matter of foods we eat. Or, should I say the foods we will not eat. A few other culture value clashes occur in time orientation, views of space, and solving problems. Overcoming cultural value challenge requires making a drastic personal reorientation of our own values.

Challenge of living within our own little cocoons, not venturing out or listening to where and to whom God wants us to go. Culture tricks us into forming patterns in life so that subtly these patterns become just a natural part of who we are, what we value, and how we behave.

In other words, culture creates walls around us that thwart us from engaging people different from ourselves. I once heard that culture is like a straight-jacket that fits comfortably. Living within our own culture we become comfortable with where we shop, where we eat, etc. Then when it comes to venturing out we are not comfortable just because those places are different. This leads us to another challenge in engaging people groups.

Becoming comfortable within our social networks. Not only does culture trick us so that we build walls of where we will go, it also deceives us so we avoid forming relationships with people that are different from our background. Discipline 3 addressed this challenge and recurring trick of culture.

Fear sometimes grips so tight that we hesitate to engage people groups. In Genesis, the scripture does not indicate that Abraham feared going to another land and another people. As soon as Abraham received the promise, he obeyed (Gen. 12:4). He did not hesitate with fear. Instead, the scripture maintains that Abraham "believed God, and it was reckoned to him as righteousness" (Gal. 3:6).

It is natural to fear another culture or people that we have not experienced or met. Often our fears are misplaced because we do not understand the other culture or people. That is the subtle trick of culture over time. It tricks us into fearing the unknowns of another culture or people different from ourselves.

I have often wondered why the Bible often says, "Fear Not". The Scripture more than 365 times speaks or alludes to fear not, one time per day of the year. Remember in the Bible when the spies returned from the land and gave their report. They reported that the inhabitants were giants and the people began to fear and complain. Are there so many passages that say "Fear not" because God knows fear is Satan's best weapon to imprison us as humans?

The love-hate relationship with dispersed people. The contemporary movement of dispersed people across national borders raises a whole range of issues. Probably the greatest issue is how migrations stimulate change in many directions: among those who move, among those left behind who often continue to communicate and maintain relations with dispersed people, and not least among those where dispersed people settle. Probably one of the greater challenges is how dispersed people affect the people where they settle. Some people react with acceptance. Others, though, react with disdain. How we deal with such local challenges is not an easily balanced tight rope.

This love-hate relationship is not new historically and has permeated every nation where dispersed people have settled. As an example, consider the sentiments that Benjamin Franklin made about Germans migrating to Pennsylvania in 1751:

> Why should [immigrants] establish their language and manners to the exclusion of ours? Why should Pennsylvania, founded by the English, become a colony of aliens who will shortly be so numerous as to [change] us instead of our anglifying them, and will never adopt our language or customs, any more than they can acquire our complexion.

Or, conversely, consider the sentiments of George Washington, 1783, addressing a group of Irish immigrants,

> The bosom of America is open to receive not only the opulent and respectable stranger, but the oppressed and persecuted of all nations and religions, whom we shall welcome to participate to all of our rights and privileges,

if by decency and propriety of conduct they appear to merit the employment.

As another example, Japan, often seen as a homogenous nation, imported Japanese Brazilians to work in factories in Japan. Japanese Brazilians, though appearing similar to the Japanese people, culturally stood out because of the way they walked, the way they sat, and the way they expressed their emotions, all of which were more casual, open, and familiar than is customary in Japan. They also spoke Japanese in a way that is noticeably imperfect, if they spoke Japanese at all. The Japanese often treated the Japanese Brazilians with suspicion, as culturally inferior, and as people whose families must have been socially and economically unsuccessful if they had to emigrate from Japan in the first place. They were sometimes mocked as "country bumpkins" on television shows. As a result of their experiences, the Japanese Brazilians who migrated to Japan ended up emphasizing their Brazilian, rather than their Japanese, identity. In Brazil they emphasized their Japanese-ness, rarely participating in events such as Mardi Gras parades. Once in Japan, however, it was clear that they had also acquired Brazilian culture, which they came to embrace and exhibit with pride. Japanese Brazilians began celebrating the annual Mardi Gras parade in Japan, complete with costumes and music.

People on the Move. Last but not least, as the word itself suggests, dispersed peoples are often on the move. When we look at the sheer numbers of how nations throughout the world are being changed due to the dispersion of peoples, we wonder if it is even quite possible to accomplish the task of reaching them.

The United States, long considered the preeminent immigrant nation, is now but one among many nations home to dispersed peoples and where people are moving. A few of those nations (United Nations Department of Economic and Social Affairs 2015), include ...

Nation	Foreign Born %	Ratio to Total Population
Australia	27.7	1 to 3.6
Canada	21.9	1 to 4.6
Estonia	16.5	1 to 6.1
Ireland	15.9	1 to 6.3
Germany	14.9	1 to 6.7
Sweden	14.3	1 to 7.0
United States	14.3	1 to 7.0
Spain	14.0	1 to 7.1
United Kingdom	13.2	1 to 7.6
Belgium	12.9	1 to 7.8
Ukraine	11.4	1 to 8.8
France	11.1	1 to 9.0
Netherlands	11.1	1 to 9.0
Greece	11.1	1 to 9.0
Denmark	9.0	1 to 11.1
Italy	8.3	1 to 12.0
Russia	7.7	1 to 13.0
Portugal	7.5	1 to 13.3

The United States remains home to the largest immigrant population in the world at more than 46 million, followed by Germany at 12 million, Russia at 11.6 million, Saudi Arabia at 10.2 million, United Kingdom at 8.5 million, Canada at 7.8 million, France at 7.8 million, Australia at 6.8 million, and Spain at 5.9 million. Noteworthy is the United Arab Emirates, which hosted a little over 2.4 million immigrants in 1995, now has over 8.1 million.

According the United Nations, "In Europe, Northern America and Oceania, international migrants account for at least 10% of the total population. By contrast, in Africa, Asia, and Latin America and the Caribbean, fewer than 2% the population are international migrants." (2015)

Dispersed people, people living in another country other than the one of their birth, grew by over 41% since 2000 to 244 million, or about 3.3% of the world population. This would equate to the diaspora people being the 5th largest country in the world, directly behind China, India, United States, Indonesia and in front of Brazil, Pakistan, Nigeria, and Bangladesh.

Nations with the world's largest number of dispersed peoples include ...

Nation	Total Dispersed Population (in millions)
India	15.6
Mexico	12.3
Russia	10.6
China	9.5
Bangladesh	7.2
Pakistan	5.9
Ukraine	5.8
Philippines	5.3
Syria	5.0
United Kingdom	4.9

The above data is not exact. In countries that especially dislike migrants, like the US and Europe, numbers are often underreported. Still, the above data is a very good indication of the general trends. The signs point to the number of people becoming dispersed continuing to increase. No nation is untouched from the resettling of people and the diaspora people.

THE SHEER MAGNITUDE OF THE
MOVEMENT OF PEOPLE IN THE WORLD
TODAY AND THE YEARS TO COME
MAKES DISPERSED PEOPLE A TOPIC OF
LONG-TERM INTEREST, ESPECIALLY
FOR THE CHRISTIANS AND THE
CHURCH.

What a challenge lies before us? As previously mentioned, if we counted the diaspora people as a country of their own, they would be the 5th largest country in the world. More than that, they would be a diverse country consisting of every major and minor religion in the world. They also would consist of people that call two nations their home.

Throughout history cross-cultural workers have encountered challenges. Challenges tested their faith yet at the same time sharpened their sense of being on mission for God. God who calls us also promises to "never leave nor forsake" (Matthew 28:20, ESV) us no matter the challenge that lies before us.

REFERENCES CITED

Allen, Matthew. (2002). "Therapies of Resistance? Yuta, Help-Seeking, and Identity in Okinawa." Critical Asian Studies. 34/2 (June): 221-42.

Gesteland, Richard R. (2002). Cross-Cultural Business Behavior. Copenhagen, Denmark: Copenhagen Business School Press.

Lie, John. (1995). "From international migration o transnational diaspora." Contemporary Sociology. Vol. 24, No. 4, pp. 303-306.

Merriam-Webster Dictionary. (2007). "Worldview." http://www.m-w.com/cgi-bin/dictionary?book=Dictionary&va=weltanschauung

Negishi, Mayumi. (2000). "Animistic Rituals Run Deep in Okinawa." The Japan Times Online. 17 July.

Nida, Eugene A. (1954). Customs and Cultures. New York: Harper and Row Publishers.

Okinawa Prefecture Government. (2003). "Wonder Okinawa: Festivals and Rituals of Okinawa." Http://www.wonder-okinawa.jp/022/en/ Okinawa Prefecture Government. 7 June 2007.

Oshiro, Manabu. (2004). "Ceremonial Spaces and Traditional Performing Arts in Okinawa." Http://www.jpf.go.jp/e/culture/news/0412/img/pdf/rep

ort11.pdf Japan Foundation Okinawa International Forum: Utaki in Okinawa and Sacred Spaces in Asia: Community Development and Cultural Heritage. 8 June 2007.

Payne, JD. (2012). Strangers Next Door: Immigration, Migration and Mission. InterVarsity Press: Downers Grove, Illinois.

Ryukyu Cultural Archives: Okinawa Prefectural Board of Education. (2007). "Folk Customs of the Ryukyus." Http://rca.open.ed.jp/web_e/city-2000/outline/index.html 7 June 2007.

Safran, William. (1991). "Diaspora in Modern Societies: Myths of homeland and return." Diaspora. Vol. 1, No. 1, pp. 83-99.

Tenney, Merrill. (1981). The Expositor's Bible Commentary. Vol. 9. Frank Gaebelein, ed. Grand Rapids, MI: Zondervan.

United Nations Department of Economic and Social Affairs. (2015). "Trends in International Migrant Stock: The 2015 Revision".

Wallace, A.F.C. (1970). Culture and Personality. New York: Random House.

Made in the USA
Lexington, KY
15 February 2018